TRANZLATY

Lingua est pro omnibus

Language is for everyone

Aladdin et Mirabilis Lamp

Aladdin and the Wonderful Lamp

Antoine Galland

Latin / English

Copyright © 2025 Tranzlaty
All rights reserved
Published by Tranzlaty
ISBN: 978-1-83566-963-1
Original text by Antoine Galland
From *"Les mille et une nuits"*
First published in French in 1704
Taken from The Blue Fairy Book
Collected and translated by Andrew Lang
www.tranzlaty.com

Olim vixit sartor pauper
Once upon a time there lived a poor tailor
pauper sartor habebat filium nomine Aladdin
this poor tailor had a son called Aladdin
Aladdin erat incautus, puer ignavus, qui nihil faciebat
Aladdin was a careless, idle boy who did nothing
quamquam totum diem ludere faciebat
although, he did like to play ball all day long
hoc fecit in plateis cum aliis pueris otiosis
this he did in the streets with other little idle boys
Is adeo contristatus est patri ut moreretur
This so grieved the father that he died
mater eius et oravit et nihil profuit
his mother cried and prayed, but nothing helped
non obstante deprecando, Aladdin vias suas non emendavit
despite her pleading, Aladdin did not mend his ways
Uno die, Aladdin in plateis ludebat more solito
One day, Aladdin was playing in the streets, as usual
extraneus interrogavit eum aetatis suae
a stranger asked him his age
Et interrogabat eum: " Nonne tu es filius Mustaphae sartoris?
and he asked him, "are you not the son of Mustapha the tailor?"
Respondit : Filius Mustaphae, domine, ego sum
"I am the son of Mustapha, sir," replied Aladdin
"sed diu ante mortuus est"
"but he died a long time ago"
advena celebre African magus
the stranger was a famous African magician
Et cecidit super collum eius et osculatus est eum
and he fell on his neck and kissed him
"Pater tuus sum", dixit magus
"I am your uncle," said the magician
"Scivi te ex similitudine fratris mei";
"I knew you from your likeness to my brother"
"Vade ad matrem tuam et dic ei quod venio".

"Go to your mother and tell her I am coming"
Aladdin cucurrit domum suam et nuntiavit matri suae nuper inventae avunculi sui
Aladdin ran home and told his mother of his newly found uncle
"Immo puer", inquit, "pater tuus frater erat";
"Indeed, child," she said, "your father had a brother"
"sed semper putavi eum mortuum esse".
"but I always thought he was dead"
Sed cenam paravit visitatori
However, she prepared supper for the visitor
et Aladdin avunculum suum quaerere iussit
and she bade Aladdin to seek his uncle
avunculus Aladdin cum vino et pomis onustus
Aladdin's uncle came laden with wine and fruit
Decidit et osculatus est locum in quo Mustaphae sedere solebat
He fell down and kissed the place where Mustapha used to sit
iubetque Aladdin matrem ne mireris
and he bid Aladdin's mother not to be surprised
exposuit se quadraginta annos e regione fuisse
he explained he had been out of the country for forty years
Qui conversus ad Aladdin et percontatus negotiationem suam
He then turned to Aladdin and asked him his trade
sed puer pudore caput pependerat
but the boy hung his head in shame
et mater eius in lacrimas
and his mother burst into tears
ita Aladdin patrui obtulit cibum
so Aladdin's uncle offered to provide food

Postero die Aladdin pulchre vestes emit
The next day he bought Aladdin a fine set of clothes
et cepit eum totam civitatem
and he took him all over the city
spectaculum urbis ei ostendit

he showed him the sights of the city
nocte perduxit ad matrem
at nightfall he brought him home to his mother
mater gavisa est videre filium tam bene vestitum
his mother was overjoyed to see her son so well dressed
Sequenti die magus Aladdin in hortos pulcherrimos duxit
The next day the magician led Aladdin into some beautiful gardens
Longum iter hoc fuit extra portam civitatis
this was a long way outside the city gates
Sederunt ad fontem
They sat down by a fountain
et magus traxit placentam de cingulo suo
and the magician pulled a cake from his girdle
placentam inter utrumque divisit
he divided the cake between the two of them
Inde profecti usque ad montana paene adibant
Then they journeyed onward till they almost reached the mountains
Aladdin tam fessus erat ut redire oraret
Aladdin was so tired that he begged to go back
sed magus eum blandis fabulis decepit
but the magician beguiled him with pleasant stories
duxit invito segnitiem
and he led him on in spite of his laziness
Tandem venerunt ad duos montes
At last they came to two mountains
duo montes angusta valle distinebantur
the two mountains were divided by a narrow valley
"Non ibimus ultra," dixit falsus avunculus
"We will go no farther," said the false uncle
"Ego ostendam tibi aliquid mirabile"
"I will show you something wonderful"
ligna colliga, dum accendo ignem.
"gather up sticks, while I kindle a fire"
Ignis accenso magus in pulverem proiecit
When the fire was lit the magician threw a powder on it

et dixit de magicis verbis
and he said some magical words
Contremuit terra modicum et aperuit coram eis
The earth trembled a little and opened in front of them
quadrata plana lapis se revelavit
a square flat stone revealed itself
In medio autem lapidis erat anulus aereus
and in the middle of the stone was a brass ring
Aladdin conatus fugere
Aladdin tried to run away
sed magus eum comprehendit
but the magician caught him
et alapam dedit ei pulsans eum
and he gave him a blow that knocked him down
"Quid feci, patrue?" dixit, miserabiliter
"What have I done, uncle?" he said, piteously
magus benignius dixit, "Nihil timete, sed oboedite mihi";
the magician said more kindly, "Fear nothing, but obey me"
" Sub hoc lapide thesaurus tuus est qui futurum est tuum " .
"Beneath this stone lies a treasure which is to be yours"
"et nemo alius hunc thesaurum attingat".
"and no one else may touch this treasure"
"Sic oportet facere prorsus sicut ego dico tibi"
"so you must do exactly as I tell you"
In mentione thesauri Aladdin timoris sui oblitus
At the mention of treasure Aladdin forgot his fears
anulum comprehendit, ut ei nuntiatum est
he grasped the ring as he was told
et nomina patris et avi
and he said the names of his father and grandfather
Lapis facile ascendit
The stone came up quite easily
et quidam gradus apparuerunt in conspectu eorum
and some steps appeared in front of them
"Descende," dixit magus
"Go down," said the magician
" sub pede illorum gradus portam apertam invenies " .

"at the foot of those steps you will find an open door"
"Ostium ducit in atria magna"
"the door leads into three large halls"
"Lingite togam tuam et ite per atria".
"Tuck up your gown and go through the halls"
"Vide ne aliquid tangere"
"make sure not to touch anything"
" si quid tetigeris , statim morieris " .
"if you touch anything, you will instantly die"
"Hae atria ducunt in hortum arboribus pomiferis".
"These halls lead into a garden of fine fruit trees"
"Ambula, donec perveniat hiatus in xystum".
"Walk on until you reach a gap in the terrace"
"ibi videbis lucernam accensam".
"there you will see a lighted lamp"
" Oleum lucernae effunde " ;
"Pour out the oil of the lamp"
"et affer mihi lucernam".
"and then bring me the lamp"
Annulum de digito attraxit et ei Aladdin dedit
He drew a ring from his finger and gave it to Aladdin
et dixit ei prosperari
and he bid him to prosper
Aladdin invenit omnia sicut dixit magus
Aladdin found everything as the magician had said
et congregavit quosdam fructus arborum
he gathered some fruit off the trees
et, lucernam nactus, pervenit ad os speluncae
and, having got the lamp, he arrived at the mouth of the cave
Magus velociter exclamavit
The magician cried out in a great hurry
"Festina et da mihi lucerna".
"Make haste and give me the lamp"
Aladdin hoc facere noluit donec ex spelunca esset
Aladdin refused to do this until he was out of the cave
Magus in atrocem iram volavit
The magician flew into a terrible rage

puluerem in ignem proiecit
he threw some more powder on to the fire
et alia magico
and then he cast another magic spell
et lapis revolutus in locum suum
and the stone rolled back into its place
Magus in perpetuum Persidem
The magician left Persia for ever
id plane ostendit, avunculum Aladdin's non fuisse
this plainly showed that he was no uncle of Aladdin's
quod vere erat magus callidus
what he really was was a cunning magician
magus qui legit de lucerna magica
a magician who had read of a magic lamp
lucerna magica, quae faceret eum potentissimum in mundo
a magic lamp which would make him the most powerful man in the world
sed solus scivit ubi inveniret lucernam magicam
but he alone knew where to find the magic lamp
et non potuit nisi de manu alterius accipere lampadem magicam
and he could only receive the magic lamp from the hand of another
Stultum hoc Aladdin desumpsit
He had picked out the foolish Aladdin for this purpose
lucerna magica acquirere et postea occidere eum in animo habuit
he had intended to get the magical lamp and kill him afterwards

Biduo Aladdin in tenebris manserunt
For two days Aladdin remained in the dark
clamavit et planxit statum suum
he cried and lamented his situation
Tandem prensat in orando manus
At last he clasped his hands in prayer
eoque facto anulum terit

and in so doing he rubbed the ring
magus oblitus est anulum ab eo accipere
the magician had forgotten to take the ring back from him
Protinus ingens atroxque genis de terra resurrexit
Immediately an enormous and frightful genie rose out of the earth
Quid vis ut faciam?
"What would thou have me do?"
"servus anuli sum".
"I am the Slave of the Ring"
et in omnibus obediam tibi.
"and I will obey thee in all things"
Aladdin sine timore respondit: "Libera me de hoc loco!"
Aladdin fearlessly replied: "Deliver me from this place!"
et aperta est terra super eum
and the earth opened above him
et foris se invenit
and he found himself outside
Ut primum lucem oculi ferre possent, abiit domum
As soon as his eyes could bear the light he went home
sed evigilavit cum illuc
but he fainted when he got there
Cum ad se venisset, matri narravit quae gesta sunt
When he came to himself he told his mother what had happened
et ostendit ei lucernam
and he showed her the lamp
et ostendit ei fructus quos in horto collegerat
and he showed her the fruits he had gathered in the garden
fructus erant in re, lapides pretiosos
the fruits were, in reality, precious stones
Tum cibum quaesivit
He then asked for some food
"Eheu! puer", inquit!
"Alas! child," she said
"Non habeo cibum in domo"
"I have no food in the house"

"At ego modicum bombacio carmen"
"but I have spun a little cotton"
"et ibo et vendam bombacio"
"and I will go and sell the cotton"
Aladdin iussit servare eam bombacio
Aladdin bade her keep her cotton
dixit ei se lucerna magica vendere pro bombacio
he told her he would sell the magic lamp instead of the cotton
Cum sordidatum admodum esset, magicae lucernae fricare coepit
As it was very dirty she began to rub the magic lamp
mundum magicam lucernam arcessere pluris
a clean magic lamp might fetch a higher price
Protinus deformis genie apparuit
Instantly a hideous genie appeared
interrogavit quid vellet habere
he asked what she would like to have
ad aspectum genie excidit
at the sight of the genie she fainted
sed Aladdin, arripiens lucernam magicam, audacter dixit:
but Aladdin, snatching the magic lamp, said boldly:
"Affer mihi quod manducem!"
"Fetch me something to eat!"
Reversus est genie cum cratere argenteo
The genie returned with a silver bowl
Habebat duodecim catillas argenteas cum pinguibus carnibus
he had twelve silver plates containing rich meats
et habuit duos scyphos argenteos et duos utres vini
and he had two silver cups and two bottles of wine
Mater Aladdin, veniens ad se, dixit:
Aladdin's mother, when she came to herself, said:
"Unde hoc splendidum convivium?"
"Whence comes this splendid feast?"
"Noli pete unde cibus iste venit sed comedat, mater," respondit Aladdin

"Ask not where this food came from, but eat, mother," replied Aladdin

Et sederunt ante prandium usque ad tempus cenae
So they sat at breakfast till it was dinner-time
et Aladdin indicavit matri suae de lucerna magica
and Aladdin told his mother about the magic lamp
Oravit ut venderet lucernam magicam
She begged him to sell the magic lamp
" Nihil cum daemonibus habeamus "
"let us have nothing to do with devils"
sed Aladdin putaverat sapientiorem fore ut lucerna magica uteretur
but Aladdin had thought it would be wiser to use the magic lamp
"fors nos magicae virtutum lucernae conscios fecit".
"chance hath made us aware of the magic lamp's virtues"
"lucerna magica utemur et anulo utemur"
"we will use the magic lamp, and we will use the ring"
"anulum in digito meo semper gestabo".
"I shall always wear the ring on my finger"
Qui cum comedissent omne genus quod attulerant, Aladdinus vendidit unum de laminis argenteis
When they had eaten all the genie had brought, Aladdin sold one of the silver plates
et cum pecunia opus esset, tabulam proximam vendidit
and when he needed money again he sold the next plate
Hoc dum nulla laminae remanserant
he did this until no plates were left
Et fecit aliam voluntatem ad geniem
He then made another wish to the genie
et alia bractearum genium ei dedit
and the genie gave him another set of plates
et sic vixerunt multis annis
and in this way they lived for many years

Quodam die Aladdin audiverunt ordinem soldani
One day Aladdin heard an order from the Sultan

quisque domi manere et claudere adaperta
everyone was to stay at home and close their shutters
Principem iret et ex ea balneum
the Princess was going to and from her bath
Aladdin captus cupiditate videndi faciem
Aladdin was seized by a desire to see her face
quamvis difficillimum esset faciem videre
although it was very difficult to see her face
quia ubique ibat velamen gerebat
because everywhere she went she wore a veil
post balnei ostium se abscondit
He hid himself behind the door of the bath
et rimam in foribus Aglauros
and he peeped through a chink in the door
Regina velum ingressa ad balneum levavit
The Princess lifted her veil as she went in to the bath
et vidi tam pulchram ut Aladdin statim adamavit eam
and she looked so beautiful that Aladdin instantly fell in love with her
Domum suam ita mutavit ut mater eius perterrita est
He went home so changed that his mother was frightened
Dixit ei tam vehementer amare Principem ut sine ea vivere non posset
He told her he loved the Princess so deeply that he could not live without her
et voluit eam petere in matrimonium patris sui
and he wanted to ask her in marriage of her father
Mater, hoc audito, risit
His mother, on hearing this, burst out laughing
sed Aladdin tandem persuasit ut ad Soldanum veniret
but Aladdin finally convinced her to go to the Sultan
et iret ad petitionem suam
and she was going to carry his request
Illa mappam attulit et magos fructus in ea posuit
She fetched a napkin and laid in it the magic fruits
magicae fructus ex incantato horto
the magic fruits from the enchanted garden

fructus scintillabant et splendebant sicut monilia pulcherrima
the fruits sparkled and shone like the most beautiful jewels
Et accepit fructus magicos cum suo ut placeret Soldano
She took the magic fruits with her to please the Sultan
et exivit confidens in lucerna
and she set out, trusting in the lamp
Maximus Vizier et duces consilii in palatium ierant
The Grand Vizier and the lords of council had just gone into the palace
et se posuit ante Soldanum
and she placed herself in front of the Sultan
Ille autem neglexit eam
He, however, took no notice of her
Et abiit cotidie hebdomadam
She went every day for a week
et stetit in eodem loco
and she stood in the same place
Inito consilio sexto die dixit Soldanus ad Vizier suo:
When the council broke up on the sixth day the Sultan said to his Vizier:
"Video quamdam mulierem in cubiculario audiente cotidie";
"I see a certain woman in the audience-chamber every day"
"Est semper aliquid in sudario gerens"
"she is always carrying something in a napkin"
"Voca eam ut ad nos iterum veniat".
"Call her to come to us, next time"
ut cognoscam quid velit.
"so that I may find out what she wants"
Postero die Vizier signum dedit ei
Next day the Vizier gave her a sign
et ascendit ad radices throni
she went up to the foot of the throne
et flexis genibus permansit usque ad diem Soldani quod locutus est ei
and she remained kneeling till the Sultan spoke to her
"Surge, bona mulier, dic quod vis".

"Rise, good woman, tell me what you want"
Cunctata est, itaque Soldanus omnes praeter Vizieram dimisit
She hesitated, so the Sultan sent away all but the Vizier
iussitque eam ingenue loqui
and he bade her to speak frankly
et promisit ei veniam dare de quacumque diceret
and he promised to forgive her for anything she might say
Tum illa narravit ei amorem magnum filii erga Principem
She then told him of her son's great love for the Princess
"Deprecatus sum pro eo, ut obliviscretur eam", inquit
"I prayed for him to forget her," she said
sed frustra preces meae.
"but my prayers were in vain"
"Mitatus est aliquod factum desperatum si ire nollem".
"he threatened to do some desperate deed if I refused to go"
Rogo itaque Maiestatem tuam de manu principissa.
"and so I ask your Majesty for the hand of the Princess"
" sed nunc oro ut mihi ignoscas "
"but now I pray you to forgive me"
" et oro ut Aladdin filio meo ignoscas "
"and I pray that you forgive my son Aladdin"
Soldanus percontatus est ei quid haberet in sudario
The Sultan asked her kindly what she had in the napkin
sic explicavit sudarium
so she unfolded the napkin
et gemmas Soldano obtulit
and she presented the jewels to the Sultan
Obstipuit specie gemmarum
He was thunderstruck by the beauty of the jewels
Et conversus ad Viziernum, et quaesivit, Quid dicis?
and he turned to the Vizier and asked, "What sayest thou?"
"Nonne ego Principem largiri debeo, qui eam tanto pretio aestimat?"
"Ought I not to bestow the Princess on one who values her at such a price?"
Vizier pro filio suo voluit eam

The Vizier wanted her for his own son
et petiit a Rege, ut detineret eam per tres menses
so he begged the Sultan to withhold her for three months
fortasse intra tempus filius eius ut locupletiorem exhiberet
perhaps within the time his son would contrive to make a richer present
Votum Suorum Vizier Soldanus concessit
The Sultan granted the wish of his Vizier
et indicavit matri Aladdin quod consensit in matrimonium
and he told Aladdin's mother that he consented to the marriage
at illa per tres menses iterum coram eo apparere non licuit
but she was not allowed appear before him again for three months

Aladdin fere tres menses patienter sustinuit
Aladdin waited patiently for nearly three months
Duobus mensibus elapsis, mater ivit ad forum
after two months had elapsed his mother went to go to the market
iret in urbem emere oleum
she was going into the city to buy oil
cum ad mercatum venisset, omnes laetantes invenit
when she got to the market she found every one rejoicing
et rogavit quid ageretur
so she asked what was going on
"Nescis?" responsum fuit
"Do you not know?" was the answer
"Filius Maximi Vizier est filiam Sultani hac nocte nubere"
"the son of the Grand Vizier is to marry the Sultan's daughter tonight"
Anhelus cucurrit et nuntiavit Aladdin
Breathless, she ran and told Aladdin
primo Aladdin obrutus
at first Aladdin was overwhelmed
sed tunc de lucerna magica cogitavit et eam perfricavit
but then he thought of the magic lamp and rubbed it

iterum genis e lucerna apparuit
once again the genie appeared out of the lamp
Quae est voluntas tua? interrogavit genie
"What is thy will?" asked the genie
Soldanus, ut scis, pollicitus est mihi.
"The Sultan, as thou knowest, has broken his promise to me"
"Filius Vizier habere Principem" est.
"the Vizier's son is to have the Princess"
"Meum est mandatum ut hac nocte sponsam et sponsum adducas".
"My command is that tonight you bring the bride and bridegroom"
"Magister, obedio" dixit genie
"Master, I obey," said the genie
Aladdin deinde ivit ad cubiculum suum
Aladdin then went to his chamber
satis certa media nocte genie cubile transportatur
sure enough, at midnight the genie transported a bed
et torus habebat filium Vizier et Principem
and the bed contained the Vizier's son and the Princess
"Accipe hunc virum, genie", dixit
"Take this new-married man, genie," he said
"Extra eum in frigore noctis"
"put him outside in the cold for the night"
"Tunc rursus in luce redire conjuges"
"then return the couple again at daybreak"
Sic filius Vizier e genie sumpsit de lecto
So the genie took the Vizier's son out of bed
et Aladdin cum principe
and he left Aladdin with the Princess
Dixitque ei Aladdin : " Uxor mea es " ;
"Fear nothing," Aladdin said to her, "you are my wife"
"promissum es mihi ab iniquo patre tuo".
"you were promised to me by your unjust father"
et non adveniat vobis malum.
"and no harm shall come to you"
Principem nimis timidum est loqui

The Princess was too frightened to speak
et emisit miserrimam noctem vitae suae
and she passed the most miserable night of her life
quamvis Aladdin dormivit juxta eam, et bene dormivit
although Aladdin lay down beside her and slept soundly
Hora certa trementes genies arcessita sponso
At the appointed hour the genie fetched in the shivering bridegroom
posuit eum in locum suum
he laid him in his place
lectumque deportat in palatium
and he transported the bed back to the palace
Mox venit Soldanus ut filiam suam bene mane velit
Presently the Sultan came to wish his daughter good-morning
Infelix filius Vizier exilivit et se abscondit
The unhappy Vizier's son jumped up and hid himself
et princeps non diceret verbum
and the Princess would not say a word
et contristatus est valde
and she was very sorrowful
Soldanus misit eam ad matrem suam
The Sultan sent her mother to her
"Quare non loqueris patri tuo, fili?"
"Why will you not speak to your father, child?"
"Quid accidit?" rogavit
"What has happened?" she asked
Princeps ingemuit
The Princess sighed deeply
et tandem indicavit matri suae quid factum esset
and at last she told her mother what had happened
dixit ei quomodo lectus esset in domum alienam
she told her how the bed had been carried into some strange house
et narravit ea quae in domo fuerant
and she told of what had happened in the house
Mater eius non credidit ei in minimis
Her mother did not believe her in the least

Et jussit eam considerare vanum somnium
and she bade her to consider it an idle dream
Sequenti nocte idem prorsus
The following night exactly the same thing happened
et mane princeps non loqui vel
and the next morning the princess wouldn't speak either
de Principe loquendo recusante, Soldanus minabatur caput suum praecidere
on the Princess's refusal to speak, the Sultan threatened to cut off her head
Confessus est ergo omnia, quae contigerant
She then confessed all that had happened
et praecepit ei ut peteret filium Vizier
and she bid him to ask the Vizier's son
Soldanus nuntiavit Vizier quaerere filium suum
The Sultan told the Vizier to ask his son
et filius Vizier verum dixit
and the Vizier's son told the truth
Princeps dilexit se adiecit
he added that he dearly loved the Princess
sed mori mallem quam per aliam tam timidam noctem ire.
"but I would rather die than go through another such fearful night"
et ab ea separari voluit, quod concessum est
and he wished to be separated from her, which was granted
et tunc fuit finis epulationis et gaudii
and then there was an end to the feasting and rejoicing

tunc tres menses supererant
then the three months were over
Aladdin misit matrem suam, ut Soldanum promissionis suae admoneret
Aladdin sent his mother to remind the Sultan of his promise
Stabat in eodem loco ut prius
She stood in the same place as before
Soldanus Aladdin oblitus
the Sultan had forgotten Aladdin

sed statim recordatus est eius
but at once he remembered him again
et rogavit eam ut veniret ad se
and he asked for her to come to him
Soldanus, videns suam paupertatem, minus inclinari percepit quam semper ad verbum suum servandum
On seeing her poverty the Sultan felt less inclined than ever to keep his word
et interrogavit eius consilium Vizier
and he asked his Vizier's advice
monebat ut magni aestimaret Principem
he counselled him to set a high value on the Princess
tam magno pretio ut nemo vivus venire possit
a price so high that no man alive could come afford her
Tunc Soldanus conversus est ad matrem Aladdin, dicens:
The Sultan then turned to Aladdin's mother, saying:
"Bona mulier, Soldanus promissionum suorum meminisse debet"
"Good woman, a Sultan must remember his promises"
" et promissionis meae memor ero "
"and I will remember my promise"
"Sed filius tuus quadraginta pelves auri mihi primum mittet".
"but your son must first send me forty basins of gold"
"et phialas aureas plenas esse gemmis".
"and the gold basins must be full of jewels"
"et portari debent per quadraginta camelos nigros".
"and they must be carried by forty black camels"
"et in fronte cujusvis cameli nigri debet esse camelus albus".
"and in front of each black camel there is to be a white camel"
et omnes cameli splendide vestiantur.
"and all the camels are to be splendidly dressed"
Dic ei quod expecto responsum eius.
"Tell him that I await his answer"
Mater Aladdin adoravit
The mother of Aladdin bowed low
et abiit in domum suam

and then she went home
quamquam putavit omnia periisse
although she thought all was lost
Dedit Aladdin nuntium
She gave Aladdin the message
Et addidit, " Satis diu responsum tuum exspectet."
and she added, "He may wait long enough for your answer!"
"Non quamdiu credis, mater" respondit filius
"Not so long as you think, mother," her son replied
"Multum plus facerem quam Principem"
"I would do a great deal more than that for the Princess"
et vocavit genium suum
and he summoned the genie again
et in paucis momentis advenerunt octuaginta cameli
and in a few moments the eighty camels arrived
et totum spatium tulerunt in domuncula et hortum
and they took up all space in the small house and garden
Aladdin fecit camelos ad palatium profectus
Aladdin made the camels set out to the palace
et cameli matrem eius sequebantur
and the camels were followed by his mother
Cameli ornatissimi erant
The camels were very richly dressed
gemmae splendidae in cingulis camelorum
and splendid jewels were on the girdles of the camels
et omnes circumstantes videre camelos
and everyone crowded around to see the camels
et phialas aureas viderunt camelos portantes in dorso suo
and they saw the basins of gold the camels carried on their backs
Soldani palatium intraverunt
They entered the palace of the Sultan
et posuerunt cameli ante eum in circulo semicirculo
and the camels kneeled before him in a semi circle
et mater Aladdin camelos Soldano obtulit
and Aladdin's mother presented the camels to the Sultan
non haesitavit, sed dixit;

He hesitated no longer, but said:
"Bona mulier, redi ad filium tuum".
"Good woman, return to your son"
"Dic ei quod exspectabo eum armis apertis".
"tell him that I wait for him with open arms"
Non tempus amisit in vera Aladdin
She lost no time in telling Aladdin
et iussit eum festinare
and she bid him to make haste
Sed Aladdin primum in genie
But Aladdin first called for the genie
"balneum odoratum volo", inquit
"I want a scented bath," he said
"et volo equum pulchriorem soldano"
"and I want a horse more beautiful than the Sultan's"
"et volo viginti servos adesse mihi".
"and I want twenty servants to attend to me"
"et volo etiam sex servis pulchre ornatis ut parenti matri meae".
"and I also want six beautifully dressed servants to wait on my mother"
Denique decem milia aureorum volo in zonis decem.
"and lastly, I want ten thousand pieces of gold in ten purses"
Simul ille dixit quod voluit, et factum est
No sooner had he said what he wanted and it was done
Aladdin ascendit speciosus equus
Aladdin mounted his beautiful horse
et per plateas pertransiit
and he passed through the streets
servi aurum in turbam abeunt
the servants cast gold into the crowd as they went
Qui cum eo in pueritia luserant eum non noverunt
Those who had played with him in his childhood knew him not
creverat pulcherrimum
he had grown very handsome
Quem cum vidisset Soldanus, descendit de solio suo

When the Sultan saw him he came down from his throne
novo genero complexus aperto
he embraced his new son-in-law with open arms
et introduxit eum in atrium, ubi erat convivium
and he led him into a hall where a feast was spread
eo ipso die ducere intendit ad Principem
he intended to marry him to the Princess that very day
Sed Aladdin statim nubere noluit
But Aladdin refused to marry straight away
"Primus oportet me aptum reginae aedificare palatium"
"first I must build a palace fit for the princess"
et discessit
and then he took his leave
Postquam domum suam, dixit ad geniem;
Once home, he said to the genie:
"Aedificate mihi palatium ex marmore pulcherrimo";
"Build me a palace of the finest marble"
palatium cum jaspide, achate, et aliis lapidibus pretiosis pone;
"set the palace with jasper, agate, and other precious stones"
"In medio palatii aedificabis mihi aulam magnam cum firmamento";
"In the middle of the palace you shall build me a large hall with a dome"
"Quatuor muri atrii erunt massae auri et argenti".
"the four walls of the hall will be of masses of gold and silver"
"et quilibet paries habebit sex fenestras"
"and each wall will have six windows"
et cancellos fenestrarum gemmis pretiosis collocabuntur.
"and the lattices of the windows will be set with precious jewels"
"sed una fenestra ornatum esse debet"
"but there must be one window that is not decorated"
"Ite videte quod factum est!"
"go see that it gets done!"
Palatium postridie confectum est
The palace was finished by the next day

geniis eum ad palatium novum portavit
the genie carried him to the new palace
et ostendit ei quomodo omnia mandata eius fideliter adimpleta essent
and he showed him how all his orders had been faithfully carried out
etiam vestis holoserica ab Aladdin palatio Soldani posita erat
even a velvet carpet had been laid from Aladdin's palace to the Sultan's
Mater Aladdin tunc diligenter se induit
Aladdin's mother then dressed herself carefully
et ivit ad palatium cum servis suis
and she walked to the palace with her servants
et Aladdin sequebantur eam in equis
and Aladdin followed her on horseback
Et misit Soldanus musicos cum tubis et cymbalis in obviam illis
The Sultan sent musicians with trumpets and cymbals to meet them
sic aer cum musica et plausibus personabat
so the air resounded with music and cheers
Ducta est ad Principem, quae eam salutavit
She was taken to the Princess, who saluted her
et magno honore tractavit eam
and she treated her with great honour
Princeps vale nocte dixit patri suo
At night the Princess said good-bye to her father
et in tapete pro Aladdin's aulam profectus est
and she set out on the carpet for Aladdin's palace
mater eius ad eam partem
his mother was at her side
Secuti sunt autem servi eorum
and they were followed by their entourage of servants
Illa aspectu Aladdin delectata est
She was charmed at the sight of Aladdin
et Aladdin cucurrit ut reciperet eam in palatium

and Aladdin ran to receive her into the palace
"Principem," inquit, "formam tuam propter audaciam meam reprehendis";
"Princess," he said, "blame your beauty for my boldness"
"Spero me tibi non displicuisse"
"I hope I have not displeased you"
dixit se libenter obedisse patri suo in hac re
she said she willingly obeyed her father in this matter
quia viderat se formosum esse
because she had seen that he is handsome
Nuptiis peractis Aladdin eam in aulam duxit
After the wedding had taken place Aladdin led her into the hall
magna divulgatum est convivium in aula
a great feast was spread out in the hall
et cenavit cum eo
and she supped with him
Post cibum saltaverunt usque ad mediam noctem
after eating they danced till midnight

Sequenti die Aladdin invitavit Soldanum ad videndum palatium
The next day Aladdin invited the Sultan to see the palace
in atrium intraverunt cum quattuor et viginti fenestris
they entered the hall with the four-and-twenty windows
fenestrae carbunculis, adamantibus et smaragdis ornatae erant
the windows were decorated with rubies, diamonds, and emeralds
clamavit, "Regium est unum de mirabilibus mundi."
he cried, "The palace is one of the wonders of the world!"
"Unum est quod miror"
"There is only one thing that surprises me"
"an casu una fenestra imperfecta relicta est?"
"Was it by accident that one window was left unfinished?"
"Minime, domine, consilio factum est", respondit Aladdin
"No, sir, it was done so by design," replied Aladdin

"Majestas vestra volui habere gloriam conficiendi palatii".
"I wished your Majesty to have the glory of finishing this palace"
Soldano placuit hunc honorem donari
The Sultan was pleased to be given this honour
Et misit ad aurifices optimos in civitate
and he sent for the best jewellers in the city
Ostendit eis fenestram imperfectam
He showed them the unfinished window
et fenestellas sicut caeteri ornari iussit
and he bade them to decorate the window like the others
"Domine" respondit eorum orator
"Sir," replied their spokesman
" satis gemmas invenire non possumus "
"we cannot find enough jewels"
ita Soldanus sua gemmas attulit
so the Sultan had his own jewels fetched
sed illae gemmae mox nimis consumptae sunt
but those jewels were soon used up too
etiam post mensem tempus opus non fuit dimidium factum
even after a month's time the work was not half done
Aladdin sciebant suum negotium esse impossibile
Aladdin knew that their task was impossible
iussit solvere opus
he bade them to undo their work
et iussit portare gemmas
and he bade them to carry the jewels back
genio perfecit fenestram iussu suo
the genie finished the window at his command
Soldanus miratus est iterum gemmas suas recipere
The Sultan was surprised to receive his jewels again
Aladdin visitavit, qui ostendit ei fenestram perfectam
he visited Aladdin, who showed him the finished window
Soldanus vero amplexatus est generum suum
and the Sultan embraced his son in law
interea invidus Vizier incantationis opus suspicabatur

meanwhile, the envious Vizier suspected the work of enchantment

Aladdin miti modo corda populorum vicit
Aladdin had won the hearts of the people by his gentle manner

Factus est dux exercitus Soldani
He was made captain of the Sultan's armies

et aliquot proeliis in exercitu suo vicit
and he won several battles for his army

sed ita modestus et comis fuit ut prius
but he remained as modest and courteous as before

hoc modo in pace et contentus per aliquot annos vixit
in this way he lived in peace and content for several years

Sed longe in Africa magus recordatus est Aladdin
But far away in Africa the magician remembered Aladdin

et per artes magicas Aladdin non periit in speluncis
and by his magic arts he discovered Aladdin hadn't perished in the cave

sed non periret, evasit et duxit reginam
but instead of perishing, he had escaped and married the princess

et nunc in magno honore et divitiis vivebat
and now he was living in great honour and wealth

Sciebat quod filius pauperis sartoris hoc solum facere potuisset per lucernam magicam
He knew that the poor tailor's son could only have accomplished this by means of the magic lamp

et ibat nocte ac die usque ad urbem
and he travelled night and day until he reached the city

ille certus ruinae Aladdin
he was bent on making sure of Aladdin's ruin

Cum transiret per oppidum audivit homines loquentes
As he passed through the town he heard people talking

omnes poterant loqui palatium erat mirabile
all they could talk about was the marvellous palace

" Ignorantiam meam " inquit
"Forgive my ignorance," he asked

"Quid est hoc palatium loqueris?"
"what is this palace you speak of?"
**"Numquid non audisti palatium principis Aladdin?"
responsum fuit**
"Have you not heard of Prince Aladdin's palace?" was the reply
"Regium est inter maxima mirabilia mundi"
"the palace is one of the greatest wonders of the world"
"Ego te ad palatium dirigam, si eam videre velis".
"I will direct you to the palace, if you would like to see it"
Magus gratias egit quod eum in palatium adduxisset
The magician thanked him for bringing him to the palace
Et viso palatio, sciebat eam esse a Genie Lampadie
and having seen the palace, he knew that it had been built by the Genie of the Lamp
hoc fecit illi insanus furens
this made him half mad with rage
Voluit tenere de magica lucerna
He was determined to get hold of the magic lamp
et iret in altissimam paupertatem iterum demergi
and he was going to plunge Aladdin into the deepest poverty again
Infeliciter, Aladdin octo dierum iter venationis ierat
Unluckily, Aladdin had gone on a hunting trip for eight days
hoc mago copia temporis
this gave the magician plenty of time
Lucernas aeris duodecim emit
He bought a dozen copper lamps
et misit lucernas aeris in sporta
and he put the copper lamps into a basket
et venit ad palatium
and then he went to the palace
"Novae lampades pro veteribus lampadibus!" inquit
"New lamps for old lamps!" he exclaimed
et sequebatur eum turba
and he was followed by a jeering crowd
Principissa in aula quattuor et viginti fenestras sedebat

The Princess was sitting in the hall of four-and-twenty windows
misit servum ut sciret quid esset tumultus
she sent a servant to find out what the noise was about
servus ridens rediit ita ut reginam illam increparet
the servant came back laughing so much that the Princess scolded her
Respondit servus: Domina
"Madam," replied the servant
"Quis potest non ridere cum tale videris?"
"who can help but laughing when you see such a thing?"
"stulte vetus offert se nova lucernas commutare pro lampadibus veteribus"
"an old fool is offering to exchange fine new lamps for old lamps"
Audiens hoc servus alius locutus est
Another servant, hearing this, spoke up
"Est lucerna vetus in corona quam habere potest".
"There is an old lamp on the cornice which he can have"
Hoc nimirum erat lucerna magica
this, of course, was the magic lamp
Aladdin reliquerat ibi lucernam magicam, cum non posset eam secum capere
Aladdin had left the magic lamp there, as he could not take it with him
Princeps lucerna valorem nesciebat
The Princess didn't know know the lamp's value
ridens servum iussit lucernam magicam commutare
laughingly, she bade the servant to exchange the magic lamp
accepit autem servus mago lucernam
the servant took the lamp to the magician
inquit "da mihi lucernam novam pro hac lucerna"
"Give me a new lamp for this lamp," she said
Lucerna arripuit et servum iussit ut aliam lucernam legeret
He snatched the lamp and bade the servant to pick another lamp
et derisit omnis turba coram eo

and the entire crowd jeered at the sight
sed magus parum curabat de turba
but the magician cared little for the crowd
reliquit turbam magicae lucernae ut profectus fuerat
he left the crowd with the magic lamp he had set out to get
et exivit de porta civitatis in desertum locum
and he went out of the city gates to a lonely place
ibi mansit usque ad noctem
there he remained till nightfall
et in nocte excidit lucernam magicam et attrivit eam
and at nightfall he pulled out the magic lamp and rubbed it
Mago visus est genie
The genie appeared to the magician
Et praecepit ei magus in genie
and the magician made his command to the genie
"Fer me, regina, et in sola Africa palatium".
"carry me, the princess, and the palace to a lonely place in Africa"

Mane autem facto soldanus e fenestra ad palatium Aladdin prospexit
Next morning the Sultan looked out of the window toward Aladdin's palace
et oculos terebat , ut vidit palatium abisse
and he rubbed his eyes when he saw the palace was gone
Misit ad Vizier et rogavit quid factum esset palatii
He sent for the Vizier and asked what had become of the palace
Vizier quoque prospexit et in stupore periit
The Vizier looked out too, and was lost in astonishment
Eventus iterum posuit ad incantationem
He again put the events down to enchantment
et hoc tempore credidit ei Soldanus
and this time the Sultan believed him
triginta viros misit, qui Aladdin in catenis adducerent
he sent thirty men on horseback to fetch Aladdin in chains
Et ascendentes in domum suam

They met him riding home
et ligaverunt eum et coegerunt eum pedibus ire cum eis
they bound him and forced him to go with them on foot
Populus autem, qui diligebat eum, sequebatur eos in palatium
The people, however, who loved him, followed them to the palace
facturos se nihil nocuisse
they would make sure that he came to no harm
Elatus est coram Rege
He was carried before the Sultan
Et iussit Soldanus carnificem amputare caput eius
and the Sultan ordered the executioner to cut off his head
Carnifex fecit Aladdin genua ante truncum
The executioner made Aladdin kneel down before a block of wood
oculos alligavit ne videret
he bandaged his eyes so that he could not see
et erexit acinacem ad percutiendum
and he raised his scimitar to strike
Et statim Vizier turbam vidit in atrium irrupisse
At that instant the Vizier saw the crowd had forced their way into the courtyard
scandebant muros Aladdin
they were scaling the walls to rescue Aladdin
vocavitque carnificem ut consisteret
so he called to the executioner to halt
Populus quidem adeo minatus est ut Soldanus cederet
The people, indeed, looked so threatening that the Sultan gave way
iussitque Aladdin dissolvi
and he ordered Aladdin to be unbound
coram populo ignovit
he pardoned him in the sight of the crowd
Aladdin nunc rogabat scire quid fecisset
Aladdin now begged to know what he had done
"False miser!" Dixit Soldanus, "Venite illuc".

"False wretch!" said the Sultan, "come thither"
et ostendit ei locum ubi steterat palatium suum de fenestra
he showed him from the window the place where his palace had stood
Aladdin ita obstupuit ut verbum dicere non posset
Aladdin was so amazed that he could not say a word
"Ubi est palatium meum et filia mea?" postulavit Soldanus
"Where are my palace and my daughter?" demanded the Sultan
"pro palatio non ita multum sollicitus sum"
"For the palace I am not so deeply concerned"
"sed filiam meam habere debeo".
"but my daughter I must have"
"et invenias illam, vel perdas caput tuum".
"and you must find her, or lose your head"
Oravit Aladdin quadraginta dies sibi dari , in quibus eam inveniret
Aladdin begged to be granted forty days in which to find her
pollicitus est se, si defecisset, rediturum;
he promised that if he failed he would return
et in reditu suo mortem passurus est ad placitum Soldani
and on his return he would suffer death at the Sultan's pleasure
Eius oratio a Rege concessa est
His prayer was granted by the Sultan
Et exivit tristis a facie Soldani
and he went forth sadly from the Sultan's presence
per triduum erravit insanus
For three days he wandered about like a madman
interrogavit omnes, quidnam esset in palatio suo
he asked everyone what had become of his palace
sed risit et misertus est
but they only laughed and pitied him
Venit ad ripas fluminis
He came to the banks of a river
flexo ad preces ante se dedidit
he knelt down to say his prayers before throwing himself in

Quod cum faciebat, anulum magicum fricabat adhuc utebatur
In so doing he rubbed the magic ring he still wore
Genius, quam in spelunca viderat, apparuit
The genie he had seen in the cave appeared
et quaesivit quid sibi vellet
and he asked him what his will was
"Libera me, genie," dixit Aladdin
"Save my life, genie," said Aladdin
"reduces palatium meum"
"bring my palace back"
"Quod non est in mea potestate", dixit genie
"That is not in my power," said the genie
"Solus anuli servus sum".
"I am only the Slave of the Ring"
"Lucerna magica eum quaerendum est"
"you must ask him for the magic lamp"
"quod verum esset," dixit Aladdin
"that might be true," said Aladdin
"sed potes me ad palatium ducere".
"but thou canst take me to the palace"
"Constituit me sub fenestra mea uxori meae"
"set me down under my dear wife's window"
Statim se in Africa invenit
He at once found himself in Africa
ille sub fenestra principis
he was under the window of the Princess
et obdormivit in taedio
and he fell asleep out of sheer weariness
Cantu avium excitatus est
He was awakened by the singing of the birds
et cor eius erat levius quam prius
and his heart was lighter than it was before
Videbat omnia mala sua esse amissione lucernae magicae
He saw that all his misfortunes were due to the loss of the magic lamp
et frustra mirabatur qui eum lampade sua spoliaverat

and he vainly wondered who had robbed him of his magic lamp

Quod mane Principem resurrexit quam illa Northmanni
That morning the Princess rose earlier than she normally
semel in die compulsus est ariolos pati
once a day she was forced to endure the magicians company
Illa autem durissime eum tractavit
She, however, treated him very harshly
non est ausus vivere cum ea in palatio
so he dared not live with her in the palace
Cum esset amicientes , una ex mulieribus suis prospexit et vidit Aladdin
As she was dressing, one of her women looked out and saw Aladdin
Princeps cucurrit et fenestram aperuit
The Princess ran and opened the window
sonitum fecit Aladdin suspexit
at the noise she made Aladdin looked up
Vocavit ad se ut veniret ad eam
She called to him to come to her
magna laetitia amantibus se iterum videre
it was a great joy for the lovers to see each other again
Postquam Aladdin osculata eam dixit:
After he had kissed her Aladdin said:
"Obsecro te, Princeps, in Dei nomine";
"I beg of you, Princess, in God's name"
"Priusquam aliud loquimur"
"before we speak of anything else"
"pro te et mea".
"for your own sake and mine"
"Dic mihi quid de veteri lucerna factum est".
"tell me what has become of the old lamp"
Lucerna super coronam intermisi in atrio quattuor et viginti fenestris.
"I left the lamp on the cornice in the hall of four-and-twenty windows"

"Vae!" dixit, "Innocens ego sum causa dolorum nostrorum".
"Alas!" she said, "I am the innocent cause of our sorrows"
et indicavit ei de commutatione lucernae magicae
and she told him of the exchange of the magic lamp
"Nunc scio", inquit Aladdin
"Now I know," cried Aladdin
"Mego gratias ago pro hoc!"
"we have to thank the magician for this!"
"Ubi est lucerna magica?"
"Where is the magic lamp?"
"Lucerna portat secum," Principem dixit
"He carries the lamp about with him," said the Princess
"Scio lucernam secum portat".
"I know he carries the lamp with him"
"quia lucernam e sinu pectoris sui extrahebat ut mihi ostenderet".
"because he pulled the lamp out of his breast pocket to show me"
"et vult me fidem meam violare tecum et nubere illi".
"and he wishes me to break my faith with you and marry him"
"Et decollatus es jussu patris mei".
"and he said you were beheaded by my father's command"
"Male de te semper loquitur".
"He is always speaking ill of you"
"At ego cum lacrimis tantum respondeo"
"but I only reply with my tears"
"Si perseverare possum, non dubito"
"If I can persist, I doubt not"
"Sed vim faciet".
"but he will use violence"
Aladdin confortavit uxorem suam
Aladdin comforted his wife
et reliquit eam aliquamdiu
and he left her for a while
Vestimenta mutavit primo in urbe occurrit
He changed clothes with the first person he met in town
et quodam pulvere empto ad Principem rediit

and having bought a certain powder, he returned to the Princess
Principem admittit paulum ostium
the Princess let him in by a little side door
"Pone indue vestem pulcherrimam", dixit ei
"Put on your most beautiful dress," he said to her
"Accipe magi ridentibus hodie"
"receive the magician with smiles today"
"duc ad credendum quod oblitus es mei"
"lead him to believe that you have forgotten me"
"Invita eum ut cenaret vobiscum"
"Invite him to sup with you"
" et dic ei velles vinum patriae gustare " .
"and tell him you wish to taste the wine of his country"
" Ibit aliquamdiu "
"He will be gone for some time"
"dum abierit, dicam tibi quid facias".
"while he is gone I will tell you what to do"
Audivit Aladdin
She listened carefully to Aladdin
et discedens se bene ornavit
and when he left she arrayed herself beautifully
non erat indutus sic quia urbem reliquerat
she hadn't dressed like this since she had left her city
Induit cingulum et ornatum adamantinum
She put on a girdle and head-dress of diamonds
fuit pulchrius quam umquam
she was more beautiful than ever
et magus cum risu accepit
and she received the magician with a smile
"Constitui animum meum Aladdin mortuum"
"I have made up my mind that Aladdin is dead"
" lacrimae meae eum ad me non reducent " .
"my tears will not bring him back to me"
" sic certus sum amplius non lugere ".
"so I am resolved to mourn no more"
"propterea te invitare ad cenam mecum".

"therefore I invite you to sup with me"
"sed taedet nos vinorum."
"but I am tired of the wines we have"
"Vina Africae gustare velim"
"I would like to taste the wines of Africa"
Magus ad cellam suam cucurrit
The magician ran to his cellar
et pulveris Aladdin in poculum suum ei dederat
and the Princess put the powder Aladdin had given her in her cup
Et cum rediret, rogavit eum ut biberet ad sanitatem suam
When he returned she asked him to drink to her health
et dedit ei calicem pro anima sua
and she handed him her cup in exchange for his
quo facto in signum ostensionis reconciliata est ei
this was done as a sign to show she was reconciled to him
Magus ante bibens orationem fecit ei
Before drinking the magician made her a speech
voluit laudare pulchritudinem eius
he wanted to praise her beauty
sed princeps deficiebat
but the Princess cut him short
" Prius bibamus " ;
"Let us drink first"
et dices quid postea vis.
"and you shall say what you will afterwards"
poculum ad labia sua apposuit et ibi custodivit
She set her cup to her lips and kept it there
magus poculum exhausit in faece
the magician drained his cup to the dregs
et potione consummata recidit exanimis
and upon finishing his drink he fell back lifeless
Princeps deinde Aladdin ostium aperuit
The Princess then opened the door to Aladdin
et bracchia collo
and she flung her arms round his neck
sed Aladdin rogavit eam ut discederet ab eo

but Aladdin asked her to leave him
plus tamen fieri
there was still more to be done
Et magus mortuus est
He then went to the dead magician
et lucernam accepit de vestimento suo
and he took the lamp out of his vest
genio palatium ferre iubet
he bade the genie to carry the palace back
Princeps in thalamo suo tantum duas parvas fruges sensit
the Princess in her chamber only felt two little shocks
per modicum tempus fuit domi iterum
in little time she was at home again
Soldanus sedebat in SOLARIUM
The Sultan was sitting on his balcony
amissam filiam lugebat
he was mourning for his lost daughter
suspexit et perfricare oculos
he looked up and had to rub his eyes again
palatium ibi stabat sicut prius
the palace stood there as it had before
Pergit ad palatium ut videret filiam suam
He hastened over to the palace to see his daughter
Aladdin receperunt eum in aula palatii
Aladdin received him in the hall of the palace
et princeps ad latus eius
and the princess was at his side
Aladdin indicavit ei quod factum est
Aladdin told him what had happened
et ostendit ei cadaver magorum
and he showed him the dead body of the magician
ut credatur ei Soldanus
so that the Sultan would believe him
Decem dierum festum indictum est
A ten days' feast was proclaimed
et quasi iam viveret Aladdin reliquam vitam suam in pace

and it seemed as if Aladdin might now live the rest of his life in peace
sed vita eius non tam tranquilla quam speraverat
but his life was not to be as peaceful as he had hoped

Magus Africanus fratrem minorem
The African magician had a younger brother
fortasse nequior et callidior fratre fuit
he was maybe even more wicked and cunning than his brother
Aladdin profectus est ad ulciscendum fratris mortem
He travelled to Aladdin to avenge his brother's death
ivit ad visitandam piam mulierem, quae vocatur Fatima
he went to visit a pious woman called Fatima
putavit sibi usui fore
he thought she might be of use to him
Intravit cellam suam et pugionem pectori suo posuit
He entered her cell and put a dagger to her breast
tunc dixit ei ut surgeret et faceret iussum suum
then he told her to rise and do his bidding
et si non dixit occideret
and if she didn't he said he would kill her
Et mutavit vestimenta sua cum ea
He changed his clothes with her
et coloravit faciem suam sicut eius
and he coloured his face like hers
induit velum suum, ut aspexit sicut illam
he put on her veil so that he looked just like her
postremo non obstante eius obsequio interemit
and finally he murdered her despite her compliance
ut non posset dicere tales
so that she could tell no tales
Deinde ivit versus palatium Aladdin
Then he went towards the palace of Aladdin
putabat omnis populus eum esse mulierem sanctam
all the people thought he was the holy woman
et circumdederunt eum osculari manus eius

they gathered round him to kiss his hands
et deprecabantur eum
and they begged for his blessing
Et cum venisset ad palatium, factus est motus magnus circa eum
When he got to the palace there was a great commotion around him
princeps voluit scire quid tumultus esset
the princess wanted to know what all the noise was about
itaque dixit servo suo ut prospiceret e fenestra
so she bade her servant to look out of the window
Et interrogavit eius servus quid esset strepitus
and her servant asked what the noise was all about
et adinvenit sancta mulier tumultum
she found out it was the holy woman causing the commotion
quae aegritudines eorum sanabat eos tangendo
she was curing people of their ailments by touching them
Principem diu desideratum videre Fatimae
the Princess had long desired to see Fatima
et surrexit servo suo ut peteret eam in palatium
so she got her servant to ask her into the palace
falsus Fatima oblatum accepit in Palatium
and the false Fatima accepted the offer into the palace
magus orationem pro salute et prosperitate sua obtulit
the magician offered up a prayer for her health and prosperity
Princeps sedere fecit per eam
the Princess made him sit by her
et rogabat eum ut maneret apud eam
and she begged him to stay with her
Falsa Fatima nihil melius optavit
The false Fatima wished for nothing better
et annuit reginae velle
and she consented to the princess' wish
sed et velum
but he kept his veil down
quia sciebat se aliter reperiri
because he knew that he would be discovered otherwise

Princeps praetorium ostendit ei
The Princess showed him the hall
et interrogavit eum quid de praetorio sentiret
and she asked him what he thought of the hall
"Vera pulchra basilica est", Falsus Fatima dixit
"It is a truly beautiful hall," said the false Fatima
"sed in animo adhuc unum palatium tuum cupit".
"but in my mind your palace still wants one thing"
"Et quid est quod palatium meum deest?" interrogavit principis
"And what is it that my palace is missing?" asked the Princess
"Si ovum Roc tantum e medio huius testudine suspensum est".
"If only a Roc's egg were hung up from the middle of this dome"
"Tum regia vestra foret mundi miranda", dixit
"then your palace would be the wonder of the world," he said
Post haec Regina nihil aliud cogitare potuit quam ovum Roc
After this the Princess could think of nothing but the Roc's egg
Cum Aladdin a venatione reversus invenit eam in humore pessimo
when Aladdin returned from hunting he found her in a very ill humour
quid mali esset, scire oravit
He begged to know what was amiss
et dixit ei quid esset voluptas eius
and she told him what had spoiled her pleasure
"Miser factus sum inopia ovi Roc"
"I'm made miserable for the want of a Roc's egg"
"Si id ita vis, mox beatus eris", Aladdin respondit
"If that is all you want you shall soon be happy," replied Aladdin
reliquit eam lucernam et perfricans
he left her and rubbed the lamp
Gens apparuit, jussit ut ovum Roc afferri
when the genie appeared he commanded him to bring a Roc's egg

Gens tam magno tamque terribili stridore dedit ut aula tremeret
The genie gave such a loud and terrible shriek that the hall shook
"Miserum!" inquit, "nonne satis est omnia pro vobis facere?"
"Wretch!" he cried, "is it not enough that I have done everything for you?"
" nunc autem iubes me adducere dominum meum " .
"but now you command me to bring my master"
"et vis me suspendi in medio testi istius".
"and you want me to hang him up in the midst of this dome"
"Tu et uxor tua et palatium tuum in cinerem comburi mereamur".
"You and your wife and your palace deserve to be burnt to ashes"
"sed petitio ista non venit a te".
"but this request does not come from you"
" petitio a fratre mago " ;
"the demand comes from the brother of the magician"
"Magis, quem destruxisti".
"the magician whom you have destroyed"
"Igitur nunc in palatio tuo simulata sancta mulier";
"He is now in your palace disguised as the holy woman"
"Vera sancta femina iam necatur"
"the real holy woman he has already murdered"
"Qui vult in capite uxoris"
"it was him who put that wish into your wife's head"
"Cave te ipsum, nam vult te occidere".
"Take care of yourself, for he means to kill you"
hoc dicens, genis disparuit
upon saying this, the genie disappeared
Aladdin abiit ad Principem
Aladdin went back to the Princess
dixit ei quod graue caput suum
he told her that his head ached
Sanctam Fatimam accersiri postulavit
so she requested the holy Fatima to be fetched

manus imponere posset super caput eius
she could lay her hands on his head
et capitis sui sanarentur potestates
and his headache would be cured by her powers
quando magus accessit ad Aladdin, arripuit pugionem
when the magician came near Aladdin seized his dagger
et transfixit eum in corde
and he pierced him in the heart
"Quid fecisti?" inquit principis
"What have you done?" cried the Princess
" Sanctam mulierem occidisti."
"You have killed the holy woman!"
"Non est ita," respondit Aladdin
"It is not so," replied Aladdin
"Male occidi impium".
"I have killed a wicked magician"
et indicavit ei quomodo decepta esset
and he told her of how she had been deceived
Post hoc Aladdin et uxor eius in pace habitaverunt
After this Aladdin and his wife lived in peace
Soldano moriens successit
He succeeded the Sultan when he died
multis annis regnavit in regno
he reigned over the kingdom for many years
et longo post tempore regum stirpem reliquit
and he left behind him a long lineage of kings

Finis
The End

www.ingramcontent.com/pod-product-compliance
Lightning Source LLC
Chambersburg PA
CBHW012011090526
44590CB00026B/3967